He Gently Leads

Scripture verses taken from multiple translations, including but not limited to, NIV84, NKJV

First Printing 500 copies Oct 2018

ISBN: 978-1-937363-02-4

Published by: Victoria Tecken
City of Publication: Lake City, Minnesota

Printed by Colorhouse Graphics
3505 Eastern Avenue SE
Grand Rapids, MI 49508

He Gently Leads
A Sanctuary for Busy Moms to Connect with God

Written by Victoria Tecken
Illustrated by Sara Ferrari

Love Victoria

This book is dedicated lovingly to my Mom
who never stopped praying and believing

Table of Contents

Dear Mama – Preface

He Gently Leads	1
Thirsty Land	3
Be Still and Know	5
God Called You	7
Firm in His Purpose	9
Who are You Looking For?	11
His Mercy is New Every Morning	13
Whatever is Hidden	15
God is Mindful of You	17
Slow to Anger	19
A Willing Spirit	21
He Gives You Rest	23
God Speaks	25
Sacrifice	27
The Performance of Your Life	29
Which Body Part are You?	31
The Cycle of Hope	33
You are Consecrated	35
What are Your Absolutes?	37
A Chance to be Humbled	39
A Place for Discipline	41
Get out of Your Comfort Zone	43
Put Away Your Idols	45
Behold what Manner of Love!	47
Wait for the Lord	49
Pray Boldly	51
Chosen	53
Look Up	55
What's in Your Will	57
It Does Matter	59
Kick Apathy to the Curb	61
Am I a Failure?	63
Who is Jesus?	65
Blessed	67

What's on Your To-Do List   69
Calm the Storm   71
Time Management   73
Aware of the Moment   75
It Takes a Village   77
Putting God First   79
What Kind of Prayer?   81
Struggling to Connect   83
No Record of Wrongs   85
You are a Soldier   87
Satan Loves Isolation   89
Fleeing from God   91
We Have Only Done Our Duty   93
Lead Me to the Rock   95
Know Your Why   97
The Perfect Mother   99

5 Verses to Remind You of Grace   101
Journal Pages   102
Acknowledgments   125

Dear sweet mama,

If you are tired, this devotion book is for you. If you worry about your precious babies, this devotion book is for you. If you barely have time to put your socks on in the morning, this is for you. If you fall into bed exhausted at the end of the day, hoping, praying that you did "enough", then this devotion book is for you. If you desperately need some words of encouragement from a God who loves and cares about you, put into snack size portions by a fellow Christian mama who knows where you are at, then this is for you.

This book was created as a way for you to connect with your Savior in the brief moment of time you have, at any point during the day. This book is meant to encourage and uplift you, no matter if you spend three minutes or thirty minutes reading it. Even if you are feeding a baby with a toddler clinging to your leg, tossing laundry into the dryer and kicking the Legos into a somewhat organized pile, let God have a moment of your time. He doesn't need much, and he knows just how crazy your life is.

I am writing this book from the perspective that God is a great and loving Savior who wants to gently lead you, just like our very first verse says. He loves your children oh so much... but he loves you just the same. Take a deep breath in and let it out.

Let God into the insanity of your days. Take His Word to heart and trust Him to carry you through the moments when you don't know your right hand from your left. This book is designed for you to travel through at your own pace. Don't rush it. Take it one day at a time, even if those days are spread apart. There's no such thing as "missing a day". Just pick it back up when you are ready.

I'm here with you, in the trenches, changing diapers and worrying about these precious hearts that I've been gifted with. It's a big responsibility, isn't it?

Let's quit trying to find that strength within ourselves. I know from experience that it isn't always enough. But I know a great God who has more strength, and He will freely give to those who seek Him. I love you. Let's be encouraged by God's Word together.

Love, Tori

He Gently Leads

Extended Reading: Isaiah 40:9-11, 26

The image of Christ tenderly holding a lamb close to his heart is one found in many Christian homes, churches, and books. It is a beautiful picture, and as a mother, you can take comfort knowing that your precious child is held so dearly by their Savior.

But for a moment, let's pull our attention away from the sweet lamb, because down at the Savior's side is the mother, looking to Him for comfort, strength, and guidance. Christ keeps her close to His side so He can *gently lead*. He takes us by the hand through His word and leads us through life. You are never alone with our gentle shepherd.

He also understands the love you have for your children, how you carry them close to your heart. Your Savior carries them *close to His heart*. He understands how powerful your love for them is, and as a perfect God, He loves them even more than you do.

The creator of the universe, all mighty, all knowing and eternal, reaches down and *gently leads YOU.* His power and love surround us as we take quivering steps into the journey of motherhood.

Do you trust God to carry your children better than you can? Why or why not?

Heavenly Father,
Reassure your daughter of your presence in your role as a mother. Guide her; give her clarity and peace as she cares for the children held closely to your heart. Amen.

prayer for you

1

HE TENDS HIS FLOCK
LIKE A SHEPHERD:
HE GATHERS THE LAMBS
IN HIS ARMS AND
CARRIES THEM CLOSE TO
HIS HEART;

he gently leads those that have young.

– ISAIAH 40:11 –

Thirsty Land

Extended Reading: Isaiah 44:1-5, Hosea 6:3

Imagine yourself adrift on the ocean in a small boat, hundreds of miles from land. You are dying of thirst, your throat parched under the hot sun. You are thirsty for water, for *life*. All around you, as far as you can see, there is water. On the surface, it promises to quench your thirst, to give you relief. But if you were to rely on it for survival, you would quickly realize that the salty water only dehydrates you further. It cannot quench your thirst, no matter how tempting it looks.

Now imagine someone appearing on your small boat with a bowl of fresh, clear, cool water. A gentle hand lifts your head and gives you a drink. Pours *life* into your body.

When you are "thirsty" for relief from stress, chaos, hardship, depression, or anything else that results from living in a sinful world, how often do you try to quench that thirst with earthly remedies? These are things that may promise a relief from your struggles, but in the end they only add to the problem. When we try to fill a void in our heart with earthly water, we can be lured into temptations that pull you farther away from God and toward a variety of worldly idols like gossip, wasting money, resentment, adultery, substance abuse, and others.

God offers an outpouring of His love and Spirit. His water delivers on its promise to restore life and healing. He is the *only source* of this life giving water, and He offers it freely to you.

What "earthly water" tempts you to quench your thirst?

Life-giving Spirit, you promise to pour out your mercies and love on your daughter. Keep her eyes fixed on you when the water of the world promises what it cannot give. Quench her thirst with the water that brings life and peace. Amen.

prayer for you

THEY WILL *spring up like grass* IN A MEADOW, LIKE POPLAR TREES BY *flowing streams.*

– ISAIAH 44:4 –

Be Still and Know

Extended Reading: Psalm 46

Mothers are constantly surrounded by chaos and noise. Stillness isn't something we get to experience frequently. And it is hard to listen for God when we are surrounded by life's noise. We might try to blame it on the external chaos: the kids, work, a husband, friends and family, a combination of some or all of these things and others. But those aren't the real culprit. It's the internal chaos that makes it difficult for us to hear God's voice.

When you allow the outside noise to manifest inside you as any number of distracting emotions and thoughts, it pulls your attention away from your Savior. God doesn't require stillness in order to be heard, but He commands you to "be still" for your own benefit. Being still allows you to rest in the comfort He offers you, and that is hard to do when you are focusing on your own internal noise.

God uses words of confidence when he speaks to you. He doesn't tell you to hope, to guess, or to think that He is God. *Know that I AM GOD.* He is giving you an absolute in a world of chaos, like an anchor.

Stillness looks different for everyone, but imagine God taking you gently by the hand and leading you into a meadow of fresh green grass and sunshine. You close your eyes to rest, and He tells you how much He loves you. You mean so much to Him that He was willing to suffer and die so that you could be still and KNOW that He is your God.

Almighty Father, let your daughter be still and rest in the truth that you are a great and loving God. Remind her that you have her best interests at heart and that amidst all the chaos in the world, there is peace and stillness in you. Amen.

prayer for you

What internal noise or emotions keep you from listening to God?

5

HE SAYS,
Be still,
AND KNOW
THAT
I am God

— PSALM 46:10A —

God Called You

Extended Reading: Ephesians 2:1-10

When I did the survey for this devotion book, I asked a question: What do you feel is your biggest challenge in mothering your children? One courageous mother responded with a short but powerful answer. Feeling competent.

Do you feel competent enough to mother your child? Even if your general answer is yes, I would be willing to bet there are days or moments when you feel the opposite. There have definitely been days when I have questioned God's wisdom in calling me to be a mother. Thankfully, it isn't my evaluation of my abilities that makes the decision.

What makes you qualified to be a mother? What makes us qualified to hold any responsibility in our sinful state? There's a beautiful verse in Ephesians that settles those questions. You have been saved *by grace, through faith... and this is not from yourselves, it is the gift of God.* Read that again.

You have been called to be a mother through the grace of a God who is all-knowing. Using the word competent to describe God is an insult. God created competence. No matter what your resume looks like, you've been hired. And God has a pretty great HR department.

Tell him where you are feeling incompetent. Ask him to guide you and lift you up. And remember that the Lord tells us to bring our little ones to his feet. If you have done that, you are more than competent. You are doing the work that God has asked of you.

Great Father, thank you for calling your daughter to be a mother. Remind her that both she and her child are precious in your sight. Amen.

prayer for you

According to God, what makes you qualified to be a mother?

7

FOR IT IS BY
grace
YOU HAVE BEEN SAVED,
through faith,
AND THIS IS NOT
FROM YOURSELVES,
IT IS THE
gift of God,
NOT BY WORKS,
SO THAT
NO ONE CAN BOAST.

– EPHESIANS 2:8-9 –

Firm in His Purpose

Extended Reading: Job 36:1-7

When an athlete trains for a competition, they set a goal to guide their actions. They prepare for a purpose, and if they want to do well, they stay *firm* in that purpose. They avoid distractions. Every choice they make is ruled by the goal they have set.

God has a purpose, and He shares that purpose with us. He tells us in Luke 15:7 that "there is more rejoicing in heaven over one sinner who repents than over ninety-nine righteous who do not need to repent." Christ died to save souls, and He has commanded us to share that gospel light throughout the world.

If you are asking yourself how you can follow the purpose of reaching souls, begin with your children. Their souls are precious to your Savior, as is yours. Spending time in the Word, asking God for the things you need and thanking Him for His grace and guidance, these are things that help you remain firm in God's purpose.

Your life may be filled with stress, chaos, and confusion, but keep your eyes fixed on the goal that God has set for his people. Remain *firm in your purpose*, and heaven will rejoice with you.

What can you add to your day that is a witness of faith to your children?

Mighty Father, train your daughter to remain firm in the purpose you have set. Use her life and the lives of her children and her children's children to spread your saving Word to every corner of the earth. Amen.

prayer for you

God is mighty,

BUT DESPISES NO ONE;

HE IS MIGHTY,

and firm

in his purpose.

- JOB 36:5 -

Who Are You Looking For?

Extended Reading: John 20:11-18

How many times have we looked in the mirror, criticizing what we see? Every inch of our body subjected to intense scrutiny. We linger in the places that aren't quite right. We might frown in displeasure or even disgust. There is emptiness there in the mirror as we look for something that we just can't seem to find.

Mary Magdalene stood in front of an empty tomb, looking for something she desperately needed. When she couldn't find it, she stood crying, defeated and broken. Christ stood behind her and asked "Who is it that you are looking for?" Her sorrow is evident by her heartbroken response, *"They have taken my Lord away."*

When you are looking into the mirror, are you looking for the world's vision of beauty? It is an empty tomb. Without Christ's living breath, it is cold and lifeless. Even the most beautiful woman in the world grows old and returns to the earth.

Challenge yourself to look in the mirror and smile at the woman you see. She is made beautiful in Christ, a precious daughter who is loved by a King who makes no mistakes. Your faith makes you far more beautiful than any worldly standard ever could. Because of Christ, you are enough. Because of Christ, every inch of you is *perfect* in the eyes of God. Walk with that confidence and hold your head high.

When you look in the mirror, what are you looking for?

Beautiful Savior, you have made your daughter beautiful in your image. When she looks in the mirror, fill her with the confidence of your love. Amen.

prayer for you

He asked her, WOMAN, WHY ARE YOU CRYING? *Who is it you are looking for?*

His Mercy is New Every Morning

Extended Reading: Lamentations 3:21-26

"I shouldn't have yelled. I'm terrible at this. Why can't I be a good mom like *insert name here*? I can't believe I did that." When you make mistakes as a parent, do you feel like you have to do some kind of penance? Do you hold onto that shame and frustration with yourself, sometimes for days after the incident happens?

Negative self-talk is a dark pit that swallows us up and seems to suck all the joy from a day. It is one of Satan's many tools to keep us focused inward instead of upward. A counselor once said, "Guilt and shame are two different things. Guilt is from God, and it tells you that you've done something wrong. But shame is from Satan, and it tells you, 'Because I did this, I'm an unforgiveable, terrible person.'

Satan wants you to think that. He wants you to sink into that dark pit and tear yourself apart inside. But your Savior has a very different message for you. It is good to acknowledge your mistakes. The problem is when you dwell on them and allow them to hold you back from making a change and asking forgiveness.

In another translation, this verse reads, *"The Lord's mercies begin afresh each morning."* Every single morning, begin a new day. Ask for forgiveness for the mistakes you've made, and then rest in the knowledge that you are loved. And then show that same grace and mercy to your family. Today is a new day. Every day.

> What are you holding onto that you should ask forgiveness for?

Forgiving Savior, thank you for giving us the opportunity to renew ourselves every single day. Cleanse your daughter from any shame that she is holding inside, and give her the courage to ask your forgiveness. Amen.

prayer for you

BECAUSE OF
the Lord's great love
WE ARE NOT CONSUMED,
FOR HIS COMPASSIONS
NEVER FAIL.
They are new
every morning;
GREAT IS YOUR
FAITHFULNESS.

- LAMENTATIONS 3:22-23 -

Whatever Is Hidden

Extended Reading: Mark 4:21-25

In your closest relationships, you value honesty. Secrets can be damaging. Some secrets are kept for decades. These secrets can be mistakes made, or they can be feelings and thoughts kept inside. Have you ever convinced yourself that you can keep a secret from God?

Sinful nature is very convincing. It will sit on your shoulder and whisper lies. *God won't understand. You're too ashamed. Don't admit your true feelings to God, he won't love you anymore.*

But in the verses you read, God is very clear. There are no secrets. He already knows your heart better than you do. He knows your secrets before you admit them to yourself. And He wants you to trust Him with your secrets. Not for his benefit, but for yours. Even if it is a secret that you never share with another human being, don't let it poison your heart. Speak it out loud to the Lord. Ask Him to help you share it with the right person; if that is the path you should take.

If it is easier to write it down than speak it out loud, start a devotion journal. Only use a specific format if that is helpful to you. Just pour out your heart to God on the pages. Ask Him questions, even the hard ones. And then take comfort in knowing that God already knows. And He loves you unconditionally, no matter what your secrets are.

Is there a secret that you are trying to "hide" from God?

Listening Father, you know your daughter's heart better than she knows herself. Help her let go of any secrets she is holding onto that are causing her shame or hurt. Remind her that there is neither height nor depth that your love will not reach. Amen.

prayer for you

15

For whatever is hidden IS MEANT TO BE DISCLOSED, *and whatever is* **concealed** IS MEANT TO BE BROUGHT OUT INTO THE OPEN.

– MARK 4:22 –

God is Mindful of You

Extended Reading: Isaiah 44:1-5, Hosea 6:3

God is mindful of you. The definition of "mindful" is *conscious or aware of something.* Think about the way you are mindful of your children. Your instincts toward them are protective and nurturing, which makes you hyper aware of them compared to other people. You know when their "I'm fine" and the look in their eyes don't match. You feel intense pride in their accomplishments, joy for their happiness, and sorrow when they are hurt.

In your deepest heart of hearts, isn't that one of our greatest needs? To have someone who is by our side no matter what? Someone who carries us and rejoices with us? When we look to God to fulfill that need, we get the added bonus of being close to a Savior who has taken every mistake and shame from your shoulders and washed it away. He was mindful of our needs, and not just the needs that are trivial and earthly. He saw our need for forgiveness. He saw our need for healing from the brokenness of sin. He saw our need for unconditional love.

As your Father, God is mindful of you. He is aware of your hurts, your joys, your accomplishments. He rejoices with you, and he walks beside you every step of your life. There is not a single moment or milestone that he misses.

> What great things has God done in your life?
>
> ....
> ....
> ....
> ....
> ....
> ....
> ....
> ....
> ....

Great Comforter, thank you for being mindful of your daughter. Thank you for being her safe anchor in the storm of life. May she always magnify your name and rejoice in the great things you have done for her. Amen.

prayer for you

AND MARY SAID:
MY SOUL
GLORIFIES THE LORD...
for he has been mindful
OF THE HUMBLE STATE
of his servant.
FROM NOW ON
ALL GENERATIONS
WILL CALL ME
BLESSED.

– LUKE 1:46, 48 –

Slow to Anger

Extended Reading: James 1:19-26

There she stood, up on the stool in front of the bathroom sink, her two year old hands held out to me. She smiled a huge smile, "I'm cleaning, Mama!" Foam soap covered every spare inch of the counter top... the toothbrushes, the hairbrush, the bath toys, the washcloth. It ran in huge clumps down the wood cabinets and lay in puddles on the floor.

Instead of responding calmly, I reacted out of anger. I scolded her; I said words that came from my anger to resolve the situation. She became very upset and confused.

God tells us that we should be *slow to speak and slow to become angry.* Those two pieces of advice are right next to each other for a reason. Our tongues are so easily hijacked by our feelings.

If I could go back, I would have taken a deep breath, counted to ten. I would have calmly responded to my daughter that she had done a great job cleaning, but there were better ways to do it. I would've had her help me clean up the mess, and then gently but firmly tell her that she needed to only use the hand soap for washing hands.

Often I still forget to take a moment and slow my emotions, but it helps to take a breath and mentally remind yourself, *slow to become angry.* Respond in love, even when discipline is necessary. Reacting in anger does not build up, it only tears down.

What is a process that helps you slow down your anger?

Gracious Father, help your daughter when she struggles with anger. Calm her heart and help her resolve any stressful situation with grace and kindness. Amen.

prayer for you

19

My dear brothers and sisters, TAKE NOTE OF THIS: EVERYONE SHOULD BE *quick to listen, slow to speak* AND SLOW TO BECOME ANGRY

– JAMES 1:19 –

A Willing Spirit

Extended Reading: Psalm 51:10-17

A child went to his mother and said, "Mama, I am willing to listen better, help out more, and stop arguing with you." His mother, once recovered from the shock, was overjoyed.

How wonderful would it feel if your child came to you and said those very words, expressing a genuine willingness to better their relationship with you? What parent wouldn't love to see a more willing spirit in their child? Our sinful nature tells us that a willing spirit couldn't possibly be a good thing.

King David knew that a willing spirit toward God would *sustain* him. The Merriam Webster dictionary gives the word *sustain* the following definition: *to give support or relief to, nourish.* When you genuinely ask for a willing spirit to follow God's guidance rather than relying on your own knowledge or strength, it *nourishes* you. It gives you *relief* from the stress that you face every day from things in and out of your control.

The term "give it to God" is perhaps better explained by saying, "let go of that control you think you have and let God be your relief and nourishment." Don't try to be your own Savior, because you will not succeed. Ask God to give you a willing spirit so that you can be nourished by the one who can sustain you.

How can a willing spirit offer you relief from your current stresses?

----

*Heavenly Father,
Reassure your daughter of
your presence in your role as
a mother. Guide her; give her
clarity and peace as she cares
for the children held closely to
your heart. Amen.*

prayer for you

RESTORE TO ME THE *joy of your salvation* AND GRANT ME *a willing spirit,* TO SUSTAIN ME.

– PSALM 51:12 –

He Gives You Rest

Extended Reading: Matthew 11:25-30

Restful work may sound like an oxymoron. You've probably heard a combination of phrases over your lifetime that suggests that work and restfulness are opposites. "Work before you play," or, "Get away (from the daily grind) and have a little rest and relaxation."

As a mother, rest is something you cherish. A moment to yourself in a quiet space might be a daydream. Motherhood can be chaotic and loud, and you might find yourself wishing for a moment of restfulness. People might even suggest that you take a break and spend some time for you. As lovely as that may sound, you may not always be able to drop your mothering duties and run away for a weekend retreat with your favorite tea mug. So how do you find restfulness in the midst of a bustling household?

Christ offers you a yoke, and asks you to belong to Him, to work His fields. He challenges the oxymoron and gives you His yoke so that you can have true rest. What does that mean? True rest may not always come in the form of earthly relief from your duties. But it is a rest for your weary spirit, so that in those moments of chaos and frustration, you can take a breath and remind yourself, "I am LOVED by a great God." True rest comes when you let go of the control and allow yourself to trust fully in God's love.

He is not asking you to carry your burdens alone. His yoke is light because he carries it with us.

What Bible verses or promises of Christ can you think of in moments when you need rest?

Gentle Shepherd, give your daughter the true rest that can only be found in complete surrender to you. Hold her when she is weary. Amen.

prayer for you

23

TAKE MY YOKE UPON YOU

and learn from me,

FOR I AM GENTLE AND HUMBLE IN HEART, AND YOU WILL FIND

rest for your souls.

- MATTHEW 11:29 -

God Speaks

Extended Reading: Job 33:12-18

Have you ever thought that God wasn't listening to you? Have you ever felt that you were alone in the dark, trying to make a decision or overcome a trial alone, and that God was a galaxy away? There may have been a moment when you even heard a tiny voice of doubt in your ear asking, "Is God even there?"

In the darkest moments of your life, doubt can overwhelm you. It can feel like it is you against the world, and you aren't sure where to look for relief. In our human anger, we might even say to God, "You don't care about me. You're not here. You don't understand."

In response to his friend Job's anger, young Elihu had some profound words of wisdom. *But I tell you, in this you are not right, for God is greater than man. Why do you complain to Him that He answers none of man's words?*

Humankind's thoughts and plans are tainted by time, by sin, and by a short sightedness that cannot comprehend eternity. It can be overwhelming.

God's thoughts and plans are eternal. He has known every breath you will take in your life from the darkness before time. Before the earth had even been shaped by His hands, He knew *you.* And in those darkest moments of your life, He holds you. He loves you. And He wants you to turn to Him and place yourself in His hands. No matter what darkness threatens us in this life, God is *greater than man.*

> Can you think of a situation in your life where you felt God couldn't see or hear you?

Eternal Father, your greatness is incomprehensible. When your daughter faces darkness, take her hand and pull her into your loving embrace. Amen.

prayer for you

For God does speak,
NOW ONE WAY,
NOW ANOTHER,
though no one
perceives it.

– JOB 33:14 –

Sacrifice

Extended Reading: John 15:9-17

As a mother, you are probably used to sacrifice. You've sacrificed a good night's sleep to wake up and rock or nurse a fussy babe. You've given up eating your meal when it's hot to make sure your child has enough to eat and it is cut up into appropriately sized pieces. You've traded quiet time alone to attend to the needs of someone who needs you. Being a mother is a high calling, and the most rewarding work you will ever do. You sacrifice YOU for your children by placing their needs above your own.

Our Savior made the ultimate sacrifice. God tells us that *there is no greater love than to lay down one's life for a friend.* Christ walked to his death, step by painful step, bleeding and bruised, cursed and mocked by the very people he was giving his life to save.

Throughout your life, you will be asked to sacrifice yourself for others. Laying down your life takes many forms. In essence, it means putting your desires, needs, or comfort aside and acting in the interest of someone else. This is the truest form of love. In the extended reading, Christ says that he commands you to love as he has loved.

And it has a great reward. *I have told you this so that my joy may be in you and that your joy may be complete (verse 11).* The joy that Christ gives you is a permanent possession. It is not the feeling of happiness, which can come and go. It is the knowledge that no matter what we may sacrifice in this life, because of Christ's ultimate sacrifice, we have gained eternal life.

How do you react when you asked to sacrifice things, time or comfort for others?

Loving Savior, thank you for giving your life as the ultimate sacrifice for your daughter's life. Encourage her when she is called to sacrifice others. Amen.

prayer for you

Greater love
HAS NO ONE
THAN THIS:

to lay down
one's life
FOR ONE'S
FRIENDS.

– JOHN 15:13 –

The Performance of your Life

Extended Reading: Romans 5:15-21

You cannot earn salvation. Human nature rebels against that idea, because it wants to be able to have a measurable "color the thermometer" moment. Every good deed colors in a little bit more until the picture is full, and then the reward is given. Human nature wants its performance to be applauded. And yet somehow, as Paul says in another chapter of Romans, *"the good that I want to do, I don't do... it is sin living in me.*

You may have the best intentions when it comes to living your life in a way that will be applauded. It may even be applauded by others in the world. But every good intention has the potential to stumble, to trip and fall flat on its face. Apart from the covering of Christ, good intentions are a dime a dozen.

This knowledge can be overwhelming, and even irritating. But when you acknowledge the powerful Savior standing in between you and your inability to do "good" by God's standard, you can find relief.

In our verse, we find a comforting absolute truth: **your relationship with God does not depend on your performance.** You cannot and will not win salvation for yourself. You cannot and will not win salvation for those you love. But Christ did. And he has given it to you as a free gift. That is a truly powerful performance, and our relationship with God is safe because of it.

Saving Lord, thank you for standing in the gap between your daughter's sin and her Heavenly Father's judgment. Give her a rich measure of your Spirit so that she might show your light to the world. Amen.

prayer for you

Do you do good deeds out of love for your Savior or because you are trying to "perform"?

29

BUT WHERE SIN INCREASED,

grace increased

ALL THE MORE

- ROMANS 5:20B -

Which Body Part Are You?

Extended Reading: 1 Corinthians 12:12-31

Chances are, you've thought something similar to one of the following statements: "I wish I was more... If only I could be like... [this person] is so good at X. I wish I was good at that too."

Have you ever heard the childhood song about the dancing bones? Derived from the biblical account of Ezekiel's encounter with a display of God's power, the song tells a simple version of the valley of dry bones that the Lord raised into an army. The leg bone's connected to the knee bone; the knee bone's connected to the thigh bone... etc.

You were lovingly hand made by God for a specific time and purpose. You were meant to live here and now. God knew where your gifts and soul could have the most impact. In Corinthians, Paul tells us that *God arranged the parts of the body just as he wanted them to be.*

Think about it in terms of your body. If your foot wishes that it were a hand, it is ignoring the amazing purpose it was created for. Each part is integral to the whole. Each part is vitally important to the comfort and survival of the rest.

You've been given a beautiful body and soul that is dear to the God who created you. He loves you and is proud of you as his creation. Regardless of other callings, you have been created in part for the purpose of motherhood. Your faith and nurturing guidance is invaluable in your child's life.

What gifts do you have that you can use to help others?

Father of Creation, thank you for creating your daughter for the exact moment in time that was hers. If she is struggling to find purpose, Lord, remind her of YOUR purpose and how important she is to you. Amen..

prayer for you

BUT IN FACT
GOD
HAS PLACED THE PARTS
in the body,
EVERY ONE
OF THEM,
just as he wanted
them to be.

– 1 CORINTHIANS 12:18 –

The Cycle of Hope

Extended Reading: Romans 5:1-5

Hope is powerful. It can help you win against incredible odds. It can keep your head up when you carry heavy burdens. It can even keep you alive. But if you place your hope in the wrong thing or person, it can have devastating consequences.

Did you know that God gives us an exact step by step guide to how hope works? Suffering comes in many forms, driven by a sinful world, and it often brings you to your lowest point. It will happen, Christ tells you that *in this world you will have trials (John 16:33).* It isn't a question of if, but when.

But he also shows us the way out. The great hope that will help you overcome any lowest low you face in your life. The suffering produces perseverance. The Merriam Webster dictionary defines perseverance this way: continued effort to do something despite difficulties, failure, or opposition.

When you persevere through trials, it builds character. The character that creates hope is one that follows the example of Christ. He kept his focus on eternity through every trial he faced on earth. The hope that comes from a character built on Christ's example is so powerful! It is more powerful than any hope that the world tries to offer.

And the most beautiful part about this cycle of hope is that it repeats itself. That powerful hope gives you strength when you reach the next trial. It never leaves, never dies, never stops moving forward toward the promise of eternity.

> What promises of Christ give you hope when you are at your lowest low?

> *Powerful Christ, you have given your daughter the guidance she needs to walk through life's trials with her head held high. Keep her sheltered in the hope that comes from you. Amen.*
>
> *prayer for you*

BECAUSE WE KNOW THAT *suffering* PRODUCES *perseverance;* PERSEVERANCE, *character:* AND CHARACTER, *hope.*

- ROMANS 5:3B-4 -

34

You Are Consecrated

Extended Reading: 2 Chronicles 7:11-16

Thousands of years ago, King Solomon built the greatest temple the world had ever seen, and it was consecrated in the name of the Lord. It was a place for the Lord to be with his people and for them to be close to him. It was a place of sacrifice, of prayer, and of fellowship. And God told Solomon that *his eyes and his heart will always be there.*

King Solomon's temple no longer stands, but the words that consecrated it are truer now than they ever have been. God is not limited by earthly time or ruin. After Christ's death on the cross, the words applied to the temple that was built in the heart of every believer, a place for God to live and be close to you.

In the extended reading, God says that *his ears are open to the prayers offered in this place.* In the temple of your heart, God is always ready and willing to listen to the prayers you speak, whether in praise, thanks, request, or deepest sorrow.

The word consecrated in the Hebrew root means to be *set apart*. God has chosen and consecrated you and set you apart for his special purpose. His eyes and his heart are always with you. His eyes are always with you to see you, to watch every moment of your life. He gives you a conscience so you can see when you have made mistakes. And his heart is with you to shelter and comfort you, to remind you of his love.

What is something you can praise God for?

All-knowing Father, you have consecrated your daughter's heart and life to your divine purpose. I praise and thank you for setting her apart as a unique and beautiful creation. Amen.

prayer for you

I HAVE CHOSEN AND *consecrated* THIS TEMPLE SO THAT MY NAME *may be there* FOREVER. *My eyes and my heart* WILL ALWAYS BE THERE.

– 2 CHRONICLES 7:16 –

What are your Absolutes?

Extended Reading: Galatians 2:19-21

As a mother, you are no stranger to feeling overwhelmed. From the moment your child entered this world or into your family and you fell in love with them, you've felt overwhelming emotions of all kinds. Love, joy, sorrow, worry, exhaustion, frustration, hope, and the weight of responsibility... the list goes on.

Being overwhelmed can feel like an internal hurricane. Emotions become so strong that they can tip you off your mental axis and fling you around. When these emotions are negative, that hurricane can suck us down into darker feelings of defeat or despair.

The truth is that your emotions are subject to a sinful mind. They can and they will betray you, even with the best intentions. So what is the anchor that holds you?

Absolutes. When you begin thinking of a list of things you know to be absolutely true, the list shows itself to be extremely short. We cannot even say with surety that we will live another hour. An absolute truth is the arms of a perfect God that can reach into the hurricane and not only stop the storm, but he can pull you out of it. Whenever you feel out of control and overwhelmed, what are the two absolutes that you can repeat to yourself every single time?

1. God loves you.
2. God's love for you does not change.

As simple as those two absolutes are, they are a perfect comfort. Our emotions change frequently. The world changes every second. God is the one powerful anchor that does not change, and never stops loving you.

What are true absolutes from God versus false absolutes from the world? How can you distinguish between them?

Spirit of Truth, when your daughter feels overwhelmed and out of control, reach into the storm and hold her in the truth of your perfect love. Amen.

prayer for you

I HAVE BEEN
crucified with Christ
AND I NO LONGER LIVE,
but Christ lives in me.
THE LIFE I NOW LIVE
IN THE BODY,
*I live by faith
in the Son of God,*
WHO LOVED ME
and gave himself for me.

— GALATIANS 2:20 —

A Chance to be Humbled

Extended Reading: Matthew 8:5-13

Having children is a humbling experience. Motherhood challenges us to review the fruits of the Spirit on a daily basis. But it is also humbling in a profound, beautiful way.

I sat on the couch with a child snuggled up on either side of me. We were reading one of our favorite books, and my children were eagerly focused on the colorful pictures. I could pause midway through a sentence and they would light up, finishing the words they knew by heart. When we were done reading, I kissed each of their heads and they responded by kissing my cheeks.

Those moments are humbling. In the verses above, we see a man that Jesus said had *great faith*. The centurion was a respected man, the officer for one hundred Roman soldiers. He came to ask Jesus to heal his servant, someone who was much lower in their society than the centurion. The servant obviously meant a great deal to the officer.

He came to Jesus because he trusted that his servant could and would be healed. There was no doubt in his mind that Jesus had the power to perform such a miracle. He came to the Savior in humility and confidence, because he knew he was in the presence of someone greater than himself.

Our children are blessings and gifts from the Lord. Through them, we are reminded every day that we are in the presence of someone greater than ourselves.

Find a Scripture verse (not in this book) that encourages you to trust in God.

Healing Savior, thank you for using the story of the centurion to teach your daughter the blessing of humility and trust. Help her see her children in a way that draws her closer to you. Amen.

prayer for you

39

THEN JESUS SAID
TO THE CENTURION,
"Go! Let it be done just as
you believed it would."
AND HIS SERVANT
WAS HEALED
at that moment.

- MATTHEW 8:13 -

A Place for Discipline

Extended Reading: Hebrews 12:9-12

Discipline might be one of the most difficult and painful parts of parenthood. And yet, God calls his people to discipline their children in love. No doubt you have come to one of those moments in parenting where you need to set a boundary for your child. Even though it is for their own good, they most often do not understand the bigger picture yet. This makes it very difficult for both parent and child.

It is easier to let go, to back down, and to say, "I just don't want to do this right now." But think for a moment about what your calling as a parent allows you to do for your child. In your home, your gentle but firm correction and guidance can produce *a harvest of righteousness and peace.* God created the family unit and parenthood so that children could have a safe, loving environment to be taught and given boundaries.

If you back down from setting a boundary or correcting a behavior, as hard as it may be in the moment, then they will most likely be taught by the world later. This can have devastating results, whether to your child or to someone around them. And the world's lessons can be taught with a harsh, impersonal hand.

Use your position as a parent to create an environment where you can discipline your children in a way that sets firm but loving boundaries for their protection and quality of life. If you feel yourself feeling overwhelmed or backing down from a stressful situation, take a breath, remove yourself for a moment if you need to, and ask God to give you the gentle firmness of his guiding love.

Father of Infinite Wisdom, help your daughter as she seeks to discipline her children in a way that encourages and corrects them according to your will. Amen.

prayer for you

What situations with your children do you struggle with the most?

No discipline seems pleasant at the time, BUT PAINFUL. LATER ON, HOWEVER, IT PRODUCES A HARVEST OF *righteousness and peace* FOR THOSE WHO HAVE BEEN TRAINED BY IT.

- HEBREWS 12:11 -

Get Out of your Comfort Zone

Extended Reading: 2 Timothy 1:3-7

Have you ever asked your child to do something that was out of their comfort zone? One example that many parents have experienced is introducing their child to swimming. The child stands on the side of the pool, eyes wide, fearfully looking at the deep water. Or perhaps they sit on the concrete, feet dangling into the water, stubbornly refusing any further movement.

As the parent, you know that your strong arms are capable of keeping them safely above the surface. You are right there to guide them through the fear to the reward at the end. You know that within a reasonable amount of time, they will be gliding through the water like a fish, happily splashing, diving, and swimming.

This type of fearful stubbornness to stay inside a comfort zone is certainly not limited to children. Sometimes God calls you into areas outside your comfort zone to teach us, to expand your abilities, and to help you grow.

You can see the potential and reward that awaits your child as they conquer new levels of understanding and skill. God holds out his arms for you, knowing what you may accomplish on the other side of your fear. He can keep you above the surface, and he is ready to hold you through whatever you may face. He may ask you to take steps outside your circle of what is known into something uncertain. He may challenge your fears and ask you to *trust* him.

What is something outside your comfort zone that God may be calling you to learn or experience?

Spirit of Power, thank you for holding your daughter when she is fearful of the unknown. Give her the courage to step outside her comfort zone wherever you may call her to walk. Amen.

prayer for you

43

For the Spirit
GOD GAVE US
DOES NOT
MAKE US TIMID,
BUT GIVES US
power, love and
self-discipline.

– 2 TIMOTHY 1:7 –

Put Away your Idols

Extended Reading: Jeremiah 4:1-2

In the Old Testament, God's rebuke against his people regarding idols was very clear. He *detested* the idols that his people turned to. They were lifeless pieces of a fallen earth worshipped by humans who rejected the creator of the universe because they believed their sinful knowledge was greater than God. But idols are not always as obvious as a stone statue. They manifest in common, everyday decisions that prioritize anything or anyone above God.

If you are looking for encouragement about priorities, Jeremiah may not be the first book in the Bible you would think to open. But these two verses strike at the heart of our human struggle to find anything and everything to put before our relationship with God and his will. But if God is not our first priority, then nothing else matters. It doesn't matter which earthly responsibility, family member, or accomplishment you prioritize in which order. If God is not at the very top of your list, then everything else will be dysfunctional and dissatisfying.

The Bible has a wonderful complementary verse to this devotion. *But seek first His kingdom and His righteousness, and all these things will be given to you as well.* (Matthew 6:33)

The world will always try to distract you from placing God at the top of your priority list. It will try to convince you that anything is more important. "Your to-do list really doesn't allow for a few moments of devotion or prayer" or "Your children will feel neglected if you read a verse or two from the Bible". Do not let these earthly voices pull your eyes from the true priority in your life. If God is first, everything else will fall into place.

Is there anything or anyone you are prioritizing above God?

Lord, you declare your will for your daughter in your Word. Thank you for prioritizing her salvation and giving her the opportunity to prioritize you in her life. Amen.

prayer for you

45

IF YOU, ISRAEL,

will return, then return to me,
DECLARES THE LORD.
If you put your detestable idols
out of my sight
AND NO LONGER GO ASTRAY,
and if in a truthful, just and
righteous way you swear,
AS SURELY AS THE LORD LIVES,
THEN THE NATIONS WILL
INVOKE BLESSINGS BY HIM
and in him
they will boast.

– JEREMIAH 4:1-2 –

Behold what Manner of Love!

Extended Reading: 1 John 3:1-3

Children look up to their parents for affirmation. It is in our nature as human beings to seek approval and affirmation of things we do. "Is this right?" or "Are you proud of me?" are things you might hear your children say in any number of situations.

As children grow, they seek affirmation and love from the people around them in different ways. Their experiences may temper their enthusiasm for approval, but it is still a deeply rooted desire.

Your Heavenly Father's affirmation of your value is without hesitation. The moment you doubt or hesitate, He is quick to remind you of his love. *Behold* what a great and wondrous love He loves you with! He calls you his daughter, his unique and precious creation.

The love you show to your children is strong. A mother's fierce love is mentioned several times in the Bible. Think of the desire you have to see your children overcome obstacles, to see their face light up when they have accomplished something, no matter how small. The Lord delights in his children and his love is so powerful that he has given us his name, his eternity, and his favor.

The LORD your God is with you, the Mighty Warrior who saves. He will take great delight in you; in his love he will no longer rebuke you, but will rejoice over you with singing. Zephaniah 3:17

Delight in your precious child, as the Lord Himself delights in you.

> What God-pleasing character traits do you see in your child?

Life-giving Spirit, you promise to pour out your mercies and love on your daughter. Keep her eyes fixed on you when the water of the world promises what it cannot give. Quench her thirst with the water that brings life and peace. Amen.

prayer for you

See what great love
THE FATHER
HAS LAVISHED ON US,
that we should be called
children of God!
AND THAT IS WHAT WE ARE!
THE REASON THE WORLD
DOES NOT KNOW US
IS THAT IT DID NOT
KNOW HIM.

– 1 JOHN 3:1 –

Wait for the Lord

Extended Reading: Psalm 27

"Mom, are we there yet?"

Chances are if you haven't heard this famous phrase, your child just isn't old enough to say it yet. One thing true of nearly every child is that they hate waiting. You can see their little minds just crawling with the irritation of it. When they are small, being told to wait may even result in a dramatic tantrum.

Are adults really so different? Especially in a modern world where so many of our daily tasks and comforts have become nearly instantly gratifying. Food, entertainment, conversations... but isn't it true that the best things in life are often the ones you have to wait for? The things that don't just happen with the click of a button or flip of a switch are the ones you have the fondest memories of. Your closest relationships take time to develop. An art or craft that you enjoy takes time to practice and create.

Your wise Father knows the value of waiting. Right now, you are waiting for the greatest event that will ever happen in the limits of time: the return of our triumphant Savior to earth. The earliest believers waited thousands of years for the birth of Christ. They never knew the exact moment he would appear.

Notice the word that is used in the target verse: *be strong and wait for the Lord.* It takes strength and perseverance to wait. It isn't always easy. If your prayers seem to be unanswered, *be strong and wait.* If you are not sure where your life might be going and there don't seem to be any clear directions, *be strong and wait.* The verse right before our target verse says it best: *I am still confident of this: I will see the goodness of the Lord in the land of the living.*

Do you have a hard time waiting for the Lord? Why or why not?

_____

_____

_____

_____

_____

_____

_____

Great Redeemer, thank you for teaching your daughter to wait for the things that are promised to us. Give her the strength she needs to wait for you. Amen.

prayer for you

Wait
for the LORD;
BE STRONG
AND TAKE HEART
and wait
for the LORD.

- PSALM 27:14 -

Pray Boldly

Extended Reading: Hebrews 4:14-16

When was the last time you prayed boldly? Do you ever feel apologetic when you approach God in prayer? Or even fearful?

It should be daunting for a sinner to approach the throne of God. Like King David says, *What is man that you are mindful of him?* He is holy. He is perfectly just, perfectly merciful. No one on earth has ever lived a life worthy enough that they could stand before his throne in confidence. No one except Jesus Christ.

When you pray, Jesus stands between you and the throne. As the extended reading points out, he is our great high priest, making intercession on our behalf. *Let us hold firmly to the faith we profess* is a strong reminder that you have nothing to fear. The faith you have been given through the Holy Spirit gives you the confidence to come boldly before your Heavenly Father's throne and ask Him for what you need. Pray for wisdom, for strength, for clarity. Never fear that your prayers will go unheard.

God answers with more than just yes or no. Sometimes the response is *wait*, or *trust.* But do not ever fear to come boldly and speak to God. Hesitation to speak to your Father in heaven is a temptation to doubt. Pray with confidence. Ask for things that you need to keep your faith and your family strong. Come boldly to the throne and ask God to be with your children and walk with them through every moment of their lives. Ask him to nurture their faith in him.

Coming boldly to God in prayer takes an act of faith that believes in his incredible power and ability to do anything. He delights in your prayers.

> What hinders you from praying boldly or requesting something from God?

Bold Spirit, give your daughter the courage to approach the throne of her Father with confidence. Thank you for knowing her heart and hearing her prayers. Amen.

prayer for you

LET US THEN APPROACH GOD'S THRONE OF GRACE *with confidence,* SO THAT WE MAY RECEIVE MERCY *and find grace* TO HELP US *in our time of need.*

— HEBREWS 4:16 —

Chosen

Extended Reading: Jeremiah 1:4-10

There are many verses in the Bible that talk about how God has an intimate involvement in our creation as human beings. In the Psalms, King David marvels that *you [God] created my inmost being; you knit me together in my mother's womb.*

You know the wonder of an unborn child, whether through your own pregnancy or that of someone close to you. So connected to the mother's body, a tiny, beautiful soul blossoms in its first moments on earth. That soul is housed by a body that will grow, love and be loved, and live out their life, however long.

That child is hidden from the eyes of the world for a short time, held and protected by his or her mother. Those sacred moments are watched over by God himself. His mighty hands delicately form every unique feature of every child. He breathes life into their soul and knows their future. He knows even the number of hairs on the child's head. He loves that soul so fiercely, so deeply, that he offers the gift of salvation through the blood of his own child.

You are that child. You were intimately formed by the hands of God. You were chosen and made unique and beautiful in His image for this exact time in history. And when he formed you, he had already chosen you to be the mother of another precious child. You are chosen. Your soul is intimately loved by God. And so are the souls of your children.

What has been one of your favorite moments in motherhood?

Creator of Life, thank you for loving your daughter so deeply that you formed each of her features with your own powerful hands. Remind her that her soul and the souls of her children are held dearly to your heart. Amen.

prayer for you

Before I formed you
in the womb
I KNEW YOU,
before you were born
I SET YOU APART;
I appointed you as a prophet
to the nations.

– JEREMIAH 1:5 –

Look Up

Extended Reading: Ephesians 4:9-16

Some of the hardest moments in life come with parenting. You may have spent nights in tears, feeling like a failure. You might have wondered if you would ever do or say the right thing at the right time, or if you really were the right person to carry the responsibility of raising a child. You may feel out of control, as if nothing in the world were going the way you hoped it would. A word in Scripture that might describe this deep struggle is *downtrodden*.

Someone who is downtrodden spends a lot of time looking the wrong direction. It happens when the devil reaches our emotions and tempts us to focus on our feelings. As Paul says in Ephesians, when equipped with a mature faith, *we are no longer like infants, tossed back and forth by the waves*. This can easily be applied to your feelings. They are volatile.

When you look inward toward your emotions, it is like walking a balance beam while looking down behind your feet. Or driving a car while focusing your eyes on the windshield instead of out at the road.

Whenever you feel yourself being pulled inward, imagine Christ's hand reaching down to *gently lead*, lifting your head back up. The balance beam becomes steadier, the car drives straighter. Don't look in, look up.

What verse or image can you call to mind to help you focus upward instead of inward?

....

....

....

....

....

....

....

Guiding Savior, thank you for being there to lift your daughter's eyes upward when she is struggling. Steady her heart and mind with the knowledge and faith that can only come from you. Amen.

prayer for you

55

THEN WE WILL
NO LONGER BE INFANTS,
tossed back and forth
by the waves,
AND BLOWN
HERE AND THERE
by every wind of teaching
AND BY THE CUNNING AND
CRAFTINESS OF PEOPLE
IN THEIR DECEITFUL
SCHEMING.

– EPHESIANS 4:14 –

What's in your Will?

Extended Reading: Acts 20:25-35

"Where there's a will, there's a relative," may be intended as a tongue-in-cheek attempt to lighten the mood around a typically tense topic, but it is sobering as well. When we create a will, we are committing our earthly possessions to our family and loved ones. We are leaving behind our desires and legacy.

An earthly inheritance can make you richer in terms of material possessions. It can give you ownership of a family heirloom that is precious for the memories it holds. It can also be a force for Satan to pull families apart, sow discontentment and jealousy, and turn our focus to things that do not matter to our eternal soul.

You are leaving your children an inheritance that is far greater than any material possession they could own. Through the Holy Spirit, you are able to help them build a legacy of faith that will carry them through their lives and touch the lives of every child that comes after them. They will impact not only their own families, but the lives of people that come into their life from every direction.

How do you leave them a great inheritance of faith? Your actions to nurture their belief in Christ's salvation are blessed by God and of great importance. But we have to realize first and foremost that in the end, their salvation is not won by us, but by Christ. The greatest inheritance you can give them is to *commit them to God*. Pray for them and commit their faith to Christ. Ask him to bless their faith and always keep them close to his side.

What kind of inheritance do you want to leave for your children?

Spirit of Faith, thank you for giving your daughter an inheritance of eternal salvation. Bless her child(ren) with your great gift of faith and draw them always close to you. Amen.

prayer for you

NOW
I commit you to God
AND TO THE WORD
OF HIS GRACE,
which can build you up
AND GIVE YOU
AN INHERITANCE
AMONG ALL THOSE
who are sanctified.

– ACTS 20:32 –

It Does Matter

Extended Reading: Proverbs 22:1-6

Does all the work you do to teach your children about God really matter? When we are trying to explain sin and God's forgiveness, or bouncing around outside the sanctuary of the church with a fussy baby, it's easy to lose sight of the bigger picture. The child in our arms or next to us on the couch will be an adult someday.

All of their experiences in childhood add up to the person they will become. The foundation of a house is not visible, but without it the rest collapses. Even though the concrete blocks can't be seen from the outside, they were placed there carefully by the house's builder.

Your child is placing the concrete blocks for the foundation of their "house." And even though you can't see the inner workings, your Heavenly Father can.

My five year old son was building a structure out of Duplos, and when I went up to ask him what he was making, he cheerfully responded, "It's a church, Mama." It was, complete with chairs, an altar, and a Duplo Superman figure as the pastor. Both my son and my two and a half year old daughter know immediately when we turn onto the road that leads to our church, even when it isn't on a Sunday. They excitedly exclaim, "This is the church road!"

It is making a difference. What you are teaching them now may not always be visible to your eyes, but the Holy Spirit is using all of those concrete blocks to build them a faith that will carry them through the rest of their lives. Don't give up. Don't lose sight of the big picture. It does matter.

> What building blocks in the past were laid for your faith?

Lord, you are the Master Builder who lays the foundation for the faith of your daughter's children. Bless her efforts to teach them your ways and strengthen their faith through her. Amen.

prayer for you

START CHILDREN OFF *on the way* *they should go,* AND EVEN WHEN THEY ARE OLD *they will not turn from it.*

– PROVERBS 22:6 –

Kick Apathy to the Curb

Extended Reading: Psalm 73:21-28

Let's talk about apathy. Motherhood is exhausting, don't get me wrong. There are definitely times when we need to hide in a quiet room and stare out the window for a while. But rest and rejuvenation should be just that: a short space of time that is intended to recharge us so we can reenter our calling as mothers feeling stronger and calmer.

Apathy is when you allow the days to slip away. It's hard to admit when you are being lazy, especially when you are tired and overwhelmed. In those days when you need a break, it is okay to have rest. Let go of the giant To-Do list you have looming over you and choose to slow your day down. Read a book, go for a walk, allow yourself some time to just play – all of these activities are things you can do with your children, and they will enjoy your attention.

Sometimes when our feelings don't lift us up, our actions have to do the heavy lifting. Making the choice to do something positive when you feel overwhelmed will help keep you out of the fog of apathy. My grandmother has a great saying that took me many years to adopt: When you are down, do something kind for someone else.

It's amazing how powerful that is.

What is something kind (out of the ordinary) that you can do for someone else today?

Strong Father, you created your daughter to be a soldier for your glory. Lift her spirits out of the fog of apathy and give her your strength so that she can impact the world for your good. Amen.

prayer for you

My flesh and
my heart may fail,
BUT GOD IS THE
strength of my heart
AND MY PORTION
FOREVER.

– PSALM 73:26 –

Am I a Failure?

Extended Reading: 2 Timothy 1:6-13

"I feel like I'm failing my kids." Chances are, you've either said this yourself or heard another mom express it. We set unrealistic expectations for ourselves as human mothers, and then when we fall short of those expectations we tear ourselves down. We play the comparison game. We go through 101 reasons why we haven't measured up.

That mom who runs a business on the side? She struggles with being attentive to her children. That mom who seems like the perfect nurturer? She doesn't think she does enough. That mom who works outside the home? She fears that her children don't get enough of her time. That mom who stays at home? She feels lonely. All of these mothers feel guilt. Worry. Exhaustion. Fear. They all need the guidance and wisdom of Christ.

I want you to say, out loud, "Because of Christ, I am not a failure." Even better, say it while looking in the mirror. Is it hard to look yourself in the eyes and admit that? You love your children enough to teach them about Jesus. You love your children so much that you encourage their faith. Those are mighty gifts in this sinful world.

Don't let Satan pull you into the daily trivialities to measure your success. A load of laundry left undone, a book left unread, a day spent distracted... let God pick you up off the ground and lift your eyes back up to his grace. Tell your children you love them, hug them, and tell them that Jesus loves them even more.

In what areas of life do you struggle with guilt?

Gracious Savior, thank you for holding your daughter as she journeys through motherhood. Remind her of the value you place on her work as a Christian mother and help her to focus on you when she feels like she is failing. Amen.

prayer for you

HE HAS SAVED US
and called us to a holy life,
NOT BECAUSE OF
ANYTHING WE HAVE DONE
BUT BECAUSE OF HIS OWN
purpose and grace.
THIS GRACE WAS GIVEN US
IN CHRIST JESUS
before the beginning of time

- 2 TIMOTHY 1:9 -

Who is Jesus?

Extended Reading: Matthew 16:13-20

Son of God. Prophet. Forgave our sins. Created the world. Shepherd. Died on the cross. These are some of the instant responses that might come to mind when asked the question "Who is Jesus?"

Jesus asked his disciples this same question two thousand years ago. He didn't need them to validate who he was, but it was a question meant to encourage them to express their faith. To get them to really think about who he was and what he meant to the world.

At first, they respond with the answer, *"Some say John the Baptist... Elijah... Jeremiah or the prophets..."* To them, these were names that commanded a lot of respect. They might have been trying to impress Christ or each other. They knew someone as important as these prophets of God. But who was Christ to them personally? Peter answered, *the Messiah, the Son of God.*

Who is Jesus to you? In those moments when you are struggling to keep it together, who is Jesus to you? Who is Jesus when you are trying to hold onto the reins of control? Who is Jesus to you in your role as a mother? Who is Jesus to your children?

Who do you say that I am? is a personal question. Jesus came to save the nations of the world. But he also came for YOU. He is your personal Savior. Your relationship with him is personal.

Take some time to think through all aspects of who Jesus is to you. Answer the question he asked his disciples. He wants you to know him.

Jesus, thank you for intimately and personally connecting with your daughter. Show her who you are and who you want her to be. Amen.

prayer for you

Who is Jesus to you?

"*But what about you?*" HE ASKED. "*Who do you say I am?*"

– MATTHEW 16:15 –

Blessed

Extended Reading: Proverbs 31:10-31

There are some really powerful images about motherhood and womanhood in these verses. Many mothers struggle with the desire to make use of their talents and passion during the years of motherhood, especially with young children. Somehow we feel that if there is anything competing for our time with our children, it must be a bad thing.

Verse 16 says, *she considers a field and buys it; out of her earnings she plants a vineyard.* Verse 24 continues, *she makes linen garments and sells them, and supplies the merchants with sashes.* This woman was a business owner. She was an entrepreneur. She was gifted with wisdom and discernment when it came to money management. She worked with her hands, owned a business, and managed a household. But the most important thing to note is that she *feared the Lord.* She followed his will.

She raised her children AND she used the talents she was given. And her children rose up and called her *blessed.* They didn't feel neglected or second string. They saw a woman who worked with her hands and used her gifts to benefit her family and others. Whether your gift leads you to sing in your church choir, own a business, work outside the home, or creating a godly home for your family... show your children a desire to follow the Lord and use your talents for his glory.

> When your children are grown, what do you want them to say about you?

Noble Father, thank you for blessing your daughter with talents and abilities to use for your kingdom. Help her as she manages her time with her family and seeks to follow your will with her gifts. Amen.

prayer for you

HER
children
ARISE AND
CALL HER
blessed

- PROVERBS 31:28A -

What's on your To-Do List?

Extended Reading: Matthew 6:25-34

When you plan out or think through the things you need to get done in a day, what does that To-Do list look like? It probably includes a long list of housework, keeping your family's day moving forward. That doesn't count the other to do list on the side if you work outside the home or have a business. We are always filling up our schedule with things, even if we aren't going out of our home. We can fall into a cycle of busywork.

Do you have a To Do list for your kids? Read a book. Say "I love you". Give a hug. Smile. Ask them what they think about something. Pray with them. Tell a Bible story. Do something messy and then clean it up together.

These are things that take very little time, but they often get pushed aside because of the other To-Do lists in our lives. And the To-Do list that seems to be pushed aside the most is our time with our Savior. Do you write him onto your schedule? Do you make time to pray? Not just to ask for the things you need, but to thank him for his blessings?

Making time in our day to spend time with God is more important than anything else you could put on your list. God never has to "make time" for us. He is not limited by time or space. We don't even have to be thinking of him to be in his presence. He is always with us, no matter what we are doing. So take a moment to meditate on a Scripture verse while you are doing laundry. Pray for your children while you are doing dishes. When you sit down to read with them, pick a Bible story. Integrate time with God into every part of your day. Your children will see you prioritizing your faith, and that is a powerful witness.

Write down a To-Do list for today.

Great Father, thank you for giving your daughter your time and love every moment of her life. Help her fill her days with time spent with you. Amen.

prayer for you

69

BUT SEEK FIRST
his kingdom
and his righteousness,
AND ALL THESE THINGS
will be given
to you as well.

- MATTHEW 6:33 -

Calm the Storm

Extended Reading: Mark 4:35-41

Being patient with children can be a tall order for mothers. Throw in a little sleep deprivation, a complete lack of personal space, and little to no time for recharge, and it's the perfect storm. There are moments when we would be so grateful to just lay down and take a nap.

Our children are ruled by their emotions, they are still learning how to control their feelings and how to act in a way that is God-pleasing even when they don't feel like it. To be fair, this is a lifelong lesson. Even as adults we are still often ruled by our feelings. Children will often have extreme emotional reactions to situations that to us seem inconsequential or even embarrassing.

Jesus' disciples found themselves in a storm in their boat, and woke him up from a nap after he'd had a tiring day of ministry. They couldn't handle the situation themselves. They let their fear rule them, and they frantically woke him. They sound just like dramatic children; *don't you care if we drown?*

You'll notice that Jesus doesn't react in anger. He doesn't respond to their chaos with more chaos. He simply surveys the situation, brings calm, and then he takes the time to ask them to address their feelings. He is firm with them, but still in love. *Why are you so afraid?* He was reminding them that he was in control. They allowed their emotions to overcome their trust in God.

When your children are overcome by emotions, bring your calm. Remind them that God loves them and then address their feelings with them.

When was a time you were calm in the face of a storm?

Loving Savior, give your daughter the calm she needs to help her children with their emotions. Help her guide with the same gentle firmness you showed to your disciples. Amen.

prayer for you

HE GOT UP,
REBUKED THE WIND
AND SAID TO THE WAVES,
"*Quiet! Be still!*"
THEN THE WIND
DIED DOWN
AND IT WAS
completely calm.

– MARK 4:39 –

Time Management

Extended Reading: Ecclesiastes 3:1-15

This topic is a really tough one for most moms. With hundreds of tasks and responsibilities constantly pulling at our attention, it can be overwhelming to try and organize it all in a way that allows us to get everything done.

Before looking at all of the things you need to accomplish during a day... make sure that you have the most important item checked off. Where is your focus? Are you looking at your day from a temporal view or an eternal one?

God reminds us that there is a time for everything. Even in Christ's ministry, we see his example of prioritizing his time in a way that was always focused on God's firm purpose: the salvation of souls. But even with that focus, he spent time resting. He spent time away from the crowds with his disciples. He ate and drank with friends. He spent time in prayer. He made time for all of the things that were important to him, while still keeping the eternal focus.

Why do you do laundry and dishes? How could that fit into an eternal view? Try looking at it from this perspective: the care of our household allows everyone in it to be at their best. It provides a safe, clean, re-energizing space to rest, to eat and drink together as a family.

For every task, no matter how menial, there is a time. Prioritize your day by keeping the most important pieces of your life at the forefront: God and your family. Don't let a task become so important that you lose sight of the reason you are doing it.

Jesus, thank you for giving us an example of how we are to live with a focus on salvation and the loved ones you have blessed us with. Amen.

prayer for you

How can you organize your day to focus on the most import things?

THERE IS A TIME
for everything,
AND A
SEASON
for every activity
UNDER THE
HEAVENS

- ECCLESIASTES 3:1 -

Aware of the Moment

Extended Reading: Romans 8:31-39

A few days ago, my five year old son made a paper doll and colored it with red hair. He told me that it the doll was me – a Mama Doll. It was a sweet gesture and I told him it was a lovely piece of artwork. The rest of the day was stressful. There were high emotions, struggling with temper tantrums, and ending with me feeling like a complete failure as a mom.

I sat on the couch, worn out and worn down, focused on how I was feeling. Finally, when it came time to check on our kids before going to bed, I walked into my son's room. He was sleeping peacefully on his cars pillowcase, and next to his head he had carefully placed the little white paper Mama Doll.

I sat down on his bed and cried. I had convinced myself that the day was a failure, and that I had lost connection with my kids. And even in that moment, my son still loved me and wanted to be near me.

Why do we do that to ourselves? Why do we think that a mistake can sever love so easily? There is *nothing* that can separate us from the love of our Father in heaven, no matter how many mistakes we make or how much of a failure we think we are. Our children love us so much. We love our children so much. Our love is not conditional for them.

Don't let those little moments of love pass by without notice. When your child gives you a smile, or colors you a picture, or says something sweet, make yourself stop and breathe. You will make mistakes. Don't let them take away the beauty in the moments of love.

Loving Father, you make no mistakes in your love toward your daughter. Help her hold on to your grace and the blessings you have given her through the lives of her precious children. Amen.

prayer for you

Write down a sweet moment you shared with your child(ren).

NEITHER HEIGHT
NOR DEPTH,
nor anything else
in all creation,
WILL BE ABLE
to separate us from the
LOVE OF GOD
that is in
CHRIST JESUS
OUR LORD.

– ROMANS 8:39 –

It Takes a Village

Extended Reading: Isaiah 44:1-5, Hosea 6:3

Moses had a special role as the leader of the Israelite nation after they were led out of Egypt. He had many responsibilities similar to a parent. In this particular story, his father-in-law Jethro came to him and showed him that what he was doing was too hard for him. He was trying to shoulder too much responsibility by himself. He needed to reach out and organize his time so that he was a better help to his people.

Jethro never told Moses that he should feel guilty for not being able to "do it all". He just saw the need and addressed it. He knew that Moses had a lot of responsibility on his shoulders, and reaching out for help was not only helpful, but necessary.

Many mothers have a hard time reaching out for help when they need it. If you have felt that way, you are not alone. It is important to recognize that what you are doing is a huge responsibility. It's a lot of weight to carry! The old saying "it takes a village" when raising children is true. Whether it is your family, friends, church family, or a support group... make sure you feel comfortable reaching out in those times when you really need it.

If someone offers to help you, don't feel guilty about accepting that kindness. You don't need to shoulder everything on your own. Set up an accountability partner with another mom, then reach out to each other every couple of days and see how you are both doing. Tell her how she can pray for you, and ask how you can pray for her. Having a voice of solidarity can be powerful.

> **Who can you reach out to today?**
>
> ....
> ....
> ....
> ....
> ....
> ....
> ....

Heavenly Father, thank you for giving your daughter a support network. Guide her to the people she needs, and to the people who need her. Amen.

prayer for you

YOU AND THESE PEOPLE
WHO COME TO YOU
will only wear
yourselves out.
THE WORK IS TOO
HEAVY FOR YOU;
you cannot handle
it alone.

– EXODUS 18:18 –

Putting God First

Extended Reading: Matthew 6:19-24

What is the most important thing in your life? Our first response might be, "God!" and it seems like an easy answer. But what does it really mean to put God first? If we were to be put in a situation where we had to choose between God and our children, what would we say?

It is easy to pay lip service, but as a mother with a fierce love and protective instinct toward her children, it is much harder to truly place your children second to anything. And in a marriage, your children move to third!

But what are we teaching our children if we do not put their Heavenly Father first? In the gospel of Mark, Christ gives us another understanding of this concept, *"Truly I tell you, no one who has left home or brothers or sister or mother or father or children or fields for me and the gospel will fail to receive a hundred times as much in this present age... and in the age to come, eternal life."* (Mark 10:29-30).

This isn't to say that we should put God first in the hopes of receiving earthly blessings. Christ is clear: when our heart is in the right place, the blessings will come. They don't always take the shape we hope or expect, but God is faithful to those that love him. So treasure God, and put him before your children.

In what situations are you tempted to value your children above God?

Heavenly Father, thank you for giving your daughter the great gift of earthly blessings. Help her value you first in her life, and bless her children through her example. Amen.

prayer for you

FOR
WHERE YOUR
treasure IS,
THERE YOUR
heart
WILL BE ALSO.

– MATTHEW 6:21 –

What Kind of Prayer?

Extended Reading: James 5:13-20

Is there a right way to pray? What is it supposed to sound like? Should it have a sound at all, or just be something silently thought?

Prayer is one of the most underrated gifts that God has given us. It isn't showy and it isn't something that our salvation hinges on. But what is prayer? It is a powerful and intimate connection with God, a two-way channel that leads straight to our Father's ear. Through prayer, God allows us to ask him for help when we are in need, and offers us the chance to praise him for the blessings he has shown to us.

When Jesus taught us the Lord's Prayer, he was giving us an example of a prayer that was honoring God. He humbly asked for the things he needed to keep his body and spirit whole, and praised his Father for his greatness and goodness. And perhaps the most important prayer Jesus ever taught us was this: *not my will, but yours be done.*

There are several places in the New Testament that remind us that prayer is not meant to be a show for attention. It is a heartfelt conversation between you and your Heavenly Father. In all situations, pray. We remember to pray most often in the difficult times of our lives, but challenge yourself to pray daily, as often as you think of it. Challenge yourself to PRAISE as much or more than you ASK. However, you choose to pray, if it comes from your heart and you are seeking God, it is the right way.

> Write down an answered prayer.

Lord, thank you for giving your daughter the gift of prayer. Open her heart and mouth to seek and praise you in every moment, whether in pain or joy. Amen.

prayer for you

IS ANYONE
AMONG YOU IN TROUBLE?
Let them pray.
IS ANYONE HAPPY?
Let them sing songs of praise.

– JAMES 5:13 –

Struggling to Connect

Extended Reading: Zephaniah 3:14-17

Struggling to connect with God is a difficulty many Christian mothers face. Our children can monopolize our time and attention in a way that makes it nearly impossible to focus on anything else. Our days are filled to the brim, whether you stay at home full time or not. Our spirits long for that connection with God, our faith shows us our need for our Savior's reassuring word.

Here's the most beautiful thing I can tell you in this whole book. Even when you feel disconnected with God, he is not disconnected from you. You don't need to go into a quiet room with a Bible to be connected to your Savior. That quiet alone time is an important part of our ability to recharge, but it is not necessary for God to be connected to us.

He is a part of your daily life. He is right beside you as you sit on the floor surrounded by toys or scrounge together a hodgepodge of edible items to make a last minute meal. He is holding your children when your attention is pulled away. He is in every room of your house. He is not limited by the time you spend with him.

He delights in you, and the time he spends with you. He delights in your prayers and he rejoices over you! Those are pretty powerful promises! Every moment of every day, God is connected with you. Talk to him like he is right there, because he is.

What are some ways you can connect with God even when you don't have "quiet time"?

Heavenly Father, thank you for being a part of your daughter's life. Show her your presence in every moment. Amen.

prayer for you

The LORD your God is with you,

THE MIGHTY WARRIOR WHO SAVES.

He will take great delight in you;

IN HIS LOVE

he will no longer rebuke you,

BUT WILL REJOICE OVER YOU

with singing.

– ZEPHANIAH 3:17 –

No Record of Wrongs

Extended Reading: 1 Corinthians 13:1-13

Have you ever held a grudge? Or remembered something that someone said to you that made you feel angry or sad for a long time afterward? It is so easy to do. It is easy to let negative words or actions sink in and simmer. We don't confront the feelings or the person, we just let the negativity sit inside us like a slow poison.

This section of scripture in Corinthians is a famous picture of love in its purest form. Christ gave us the perfect example of this love in his life on earth. Most of the time, it is read as one large block of text, all running together. But if you look at how the verses are structured, each sentence contains pieces that connect.

When we keep a record of wrongs, it is often because we feel *angered*. That anger leads us to be *self-seeking* in our desire for justification or revenge. When we are *self-seeking* we *dishonor others* by acting in our own self-interests and allowing our anger to rule our behavior and thoughts. Instead of seeking God for our justification, we seek our own.

Our mistake is not in being hurt by something that is said or done, but when we allow those things to dictate our thoughts and actions. Our faith should dictate them. Christ's example should dictate them.

Is there something you have been allowing to poison your heart?

Jesus, you were the perfect example of love to your daughter. Guide her heart as she lets go of things she has been holding inside and sets them at your feet. Amen.

prayer for you

IT DOES NOT
dishonor others,
IT IS NOT
self-seeking,
IT IS NOT
easily angered
IT KEEPS NO
record of wrongs.

– 1 CORINTHIANS 13:5 –

You are a Soldier

Extended Reading: Ephesians 2:1-10

When I did the survey for this devotion book, I asked a question: What do you feel is your biggest challenge in mothering your children? One courageous mother responded with a short but powerful answer. Feeling competent.

Do you feel competent enough to mother your child? There have definitely been days when I have questioned God's wisdom in calling me to be a mother. Thankfully, it isn't my evaluation of my abilities that makes the decision.

What makes you qualified to be a mother? What makes us qualified to hold any responsibility in our sinful state? There's a beautiful verse in Ephesians that settles those questions. You have been saved *by grace, through faith... and this is not from yourselves, it is the gift of God.* Read that again.

You have been called to be a mother through the grace of a God who is all-knowing. Using the word competent to describe God is an insult. God created competence. No matter what your resume looks like, you've been hired. And God has a pretty great HR department.

Tell him where you are feeling incompetent. Ask him to guide you and lift you up. And remember that the Lord tells us to bring our little ones to his feet. If you have done that, you are more than competent. You are doing the work that God has asked of you.

According to God, what makes you qualified to be a mother?

Great Father, thank you for calling your daughter to be a mother. Remind her no matter how she feels about her abilities, you have called her to teach her children about you. Amen.

prayer for you

HE TRAINS
MY HANDS
for battle;
MY ARMS
CAN BEND
a bow of bronze.

— PSALM 18:34 —

Satan Loves Isolation

Extended Reading: Ecclesiastes 4:8-12

Satan is a master of deception. He has had thousands of years to perfect his craft of leading souls astray from their Savior. If not his greatest, then certainly one of his greatest tools is isolation. It can be physical isolation, but even more powerful is spiritual or emotional isolation. If Satan can make you feel alone, far away from God or the people in your life that lift you up, you are much easier for him to attack.

Isolation can often occur by the way you choose to talk to yourself. Do you say encouraging words to yourself in silence? Or is your mind overrun with negative thoughts? wants you to think that there is no one there for you, that you are alone. But he is called the master of deception because *he lies.*

In God's Word is truth. *If either of them falls down, one can help the other up.* Don't let yourself become isolated from fellow believers who can lift you up when you are low. Have you ever said to yourself, "I don't want to reach out to this person because I don't want to be a burden to them"? That is exactly what Satan wants you to think. If you reach out for help when you need it, you are not an easy target.

God can never be isolated from you. He tells you that there is nowhere in the universe you can go that he is not. Whenever you feel isolated, call to mind His promise: *For I am convinced that neither death nor life, neither angels nor demons, neither the present nor the future, nor any powers, neither height nor depth, nor anything else in all creation, will be able to separate us from the love of God that is in Christ Jesus our Lord.* (Romans 8:38-39)

> *Spirit of Truth, protect your daughter from the master of deception and lies. Give her a discerning mind to recognize the devil's schemes so that they will not pull her away from you. Amen.*

prayer for you

What "earthly water" tempts you to quench your thirst?

IF EITHER OF THEM
FALLS DOWN,
*one can help
the other up.*
BUT PITY ANYONE
WHO FALLS
*and has no one
to help them up.*

– ECCLESIASTES 4:10 –

Fleeing from God

Extended Reading: Jonah 1:1-3

"No! I don't want to do that!" screams the toddler as she runs away from her mother. Sound familiar? Sometimes the child will literally flee from their parent in an attempt to avoid the impending responsibility.

God knew that Jonah would not die when he preached to the people of Nineveh. God knew that Jonah's obedience to God's direction would result in many souls being saved. But Jonah's human nature told him to doubt God's command and flee. Jonah thought that God couldn't possibly have his best interests at heart, and that his own decision was safer. He was so unwilling to listen to God that he literally tried to sail to the opposite end of the empire, 2500 miles away from Nineveh!

The funny thing is, Jonah ended up nearly dying because of his decision. Sitting in the belly of that big fish, waiting for death, perhaps believing that God had forsaken him completely.

But God still knew. He could see the end of the story when Jonah could not. And when he saved Jonah's life, then the Bible tells us that God commanded Jonah a second time, *"Go to the great city of Nineveh..."*

God sometimes calls us to do things that scare us, and usually it requires a change of our heart and focus. It takes trust in God's perfect love and plan to step out into the unknown. But God is with you every step of the way. He will not abandon you, and he knows something greater waits for you on the other side.

All-knowing Father, strengthen your daughter's trust in your mighty will. When her human nature tells her to doubt your faithfulness, erase that doubt and replace it with your firm purpose. Amen.

prayer for you

Is there an area of your life where you are running away from God?

91

But Jonah ran away
from the LORD
AND HEADED FOR TARSHISH.
HE WENT DOWN TO JOPPA,
where he found a ship
bound for that port.
AFTER PAYING THE FARE,
HE WENT ABOARD
AND SAILED FOR TARSHISH
to flee from the LORD.

– JONAH 1:3 –

We Have Only Done Our Duty

Extended Reading: Luke 17:7-10

I don't know how many times I've thought to myself, "I just want to be a good parent." Take a moment to consider what that statement means. If we are a good parent, is that enough? Does being a "good parent" mean that we survived motherhood? A good parent survives. A good parent provides for the earthly needs of their children: clothing, food, shelter, hygiene.

A **godly** parent goes above and beyond to nourish their child's faith. A godly parent lives a life of faith as an example. A godly parent follows the guideline of the fruits of the Spirit. A godly parent fulfills the meaning of love as laid out by Saint Paul in 1 Corinthians *(Love is patient, kind...).*

That's a lot of pressure. No human mother can ever fulfill such a huge standard! But there is another piece to this puzzle: a perfect Savior who CAN provide every spiritual need. You are not parenting alone. You have been given a calling far beyond basic duty, and God himself is there to help you. Not if, but when you make mistakes, ask God to help you refocus and try again.

You can be a good parent, but to be a godly parent, you cannot lean on your own wisdom and strength. Ask for forgiveness, seek God's Word, and show your children how to put your imperfect nature in the hands of Christ.

What is one thing you want to change in your parenting?

Perfect Father, thank you for blessing your daughter with the gift of motherhood. Lift her up when she makes mistakes and return her to rest in your love and forgiveness. Amen.

prayer for you

SO YOU ALSO,
WHEN YOU HAVE DONE
everything you were
told to do,
SHOULD SAY,
We are unworthy servants;
WE HAVE ONLY DONE
OUR DUTY.

– LUKE 17:10 –

Lead Me to the Rock

Extended Reading: Psalm 61:1-5

I sat in my car in the garage, and I felt like a hot mess. I eat junk food sometimes when I'm stressed, so I was munching a medium fries from Burger King and asking God to give me guidance. It felt like there were so many things I needed to give my attention to, and none of them were getting enough. I was drained and I was desperate for his wisdom.

I was in the middle of writing this devotion book, and felt like I had hit a road block. Writing was getting harder and harder and my mind seemed to struggle with focus. After weeks of neglecting my own devotional life, I was spiritually starving for God. I was letting my life fill up with things. My to-do list was bursting at the seams.

Trying to just "keep it together" had led me to a point where I couldn't go any further. I opened my Bible. Sure enough, a passage jumped out at me from the first page I opened. *Lead me to the rock that is higher than I.*

When we genuinely seek God's guidance, there is only one place he will ever lead us: back to him. He will always lead us back to the rock that is higher than we can reach. It is a place of surety, where we can refocus on the truth and where God wants us to be.

That rock is God Himself, a sanctuary. When we need to be grounded in His wisdom, he leads us back. If we cry out to him when our spirit is faint, he will guide us to it every time.

Write down what you've been trying to "keep together". Ask God to guide you.

Lord, you are the rock that is higher than your daughter. You are her safety, her surety, and her strong protector. Guide her back to you always. Amen.

prayer for you

From the ends
of the earth
I CALL TO YOU,
I call as my heart
GROWS FAINT;
lead me to the rock
that is higher than I.

- PSALM 61:2 -

Know the Why

Extended Reading: 2 Peter 1:16-21

In almost any business model, you are encouraged to "know your why" and be able to give the reason your mission means something to you. It sets the foundation for the rest of your branding, your approach to your customers, and the direction you choose to go with your business.

Faith should be no different. When presented with the opportunity to witness your faith, someone may ask you "Why do you believe what you believe?" It is often easier to express *what* we believe, but sharing *why* can be much harder.

Now imagine that the person coming to you and asking you that question is your child. They know that faith is important. They've heard the Bible stories and sung the hymns and songs in church. They've learned to pray. But *why?*

The Holy Spirit's work is mysterious to human nature. We don't know how he creates faith in a heart. Christ told us that some things were beyond our comprehension while we are living on earth.

The Bible doesn't need any other books or human minds to prove its validity. God doesn't need us to have a good explanation in order for him to save souls. But if someone asks you about your faith, how do you answer? What does it mean to you? It is important for your children to understand the why of what they believe, and that their faith does not *have its origin in the human will*. Their faith was not designed or nurtured by a sinful world, but a powerful God.

Spirit of Truth, thank you for creating faith in your daughter's heart. Help her as she seeks to understand the work you are doing in her life. Amen.

prayer for you

Why do you believe what you believe?

FOR PROPHECY
never had its origin
IN THE HUMAN WILL,
BUT PROPHETS,
THOUGH HUMAN,
spoke from God
as they were carried along
BY THE HOLY SPIRIT.

– 2 PETER 1:21 –

The Perfect Mother

Extended Reading: 1 John 1:5-10

You know who she is. The Perfect Mother is that woman who looks like she stepped out of a home and garden magazine, fresh as a daisy while she vacuums her already clean carpet. Her children sit around her quietly, their outfits clean and matching, while they read books and talk to each other in polite, happy voices.

When people stop by her house, she welcomes them in with a warm smile and a glass of hand squeezed lemonade and from-scratch pie that she made while the baby was napping peacefully in her crib. And don't forget that she balances all seventy-three of her commitments outside the home perfectly with motherhood.

I don't know about you, but that certainly doesn't describe most days at my house. As crazy as the Perfect Mother may sound, she is the expectation that most mothers have set for themselves. Why do we do that to ourselves?

As long as we chase after a figment of our imagination that cannot and will not ever exist in reality, we are cheating ourselves of the joy of motherhood. Not only that, but there is a temptation to ignore God's greatest gift: grace.

When you lay that burden of failing to reach an unreachable perfection at your Savior's feet, he sets you free to love and be at peace in the life you have been given.

Perfect Savior, thank you for covering your daughter's imperfection with your robe of righteousness. Give her joy in her role of motherhood. Amen.

prayer for you

What unrealistic expectations do you have of yourself?

IF WE CLAIM
to be without sin,
WE DECEIVE OURSELVES
and the truth
IS NOT IN US.

– 1 JOHN 1:8 –

Five Verses to Remind You of Grace

We love because he first loved us.
1 John 4:19

Therefore, there is now no condemnation for those who are in Christ Jesus, because through Christ Jesus the law of the Spirit of life set me free from the law of sin and death.
Romans 8:1-2

Who is a God like you, who pardons sin and forgives the transgression of the remnant of his inheritance? You do not stay angry forever but delight to show mercy.
Micah 7:18-19

Let us not become weary in doing good, for at the proper time we will reap a harvest if we do not give up. Therefore, as we have opportunity, let us do good to all people, especially those who belong to the family of believers.
Galatians 6:9-10

But he said to me, "My grace is sufficient for you, for my power is made perfect in weakness." Therefore, I will boast all the more gladly about my weaknesses, so that Christ's power may rest on me.
2 Corinthians 12:9

Journal

Journal

Journal

Journal

Journal

Journal

Journal

Journal

Journal

Journal

Journal

Journal

Journal

Journal

Journal

Journal

Journal

Journal

Journal

Journal

Journal

Journal

Journal

Acknowledgments

I cannot end this book without drawing attention to the incredible support network I have had in writing it:

To my Heavenly Father, who has redeemed me and brought me out of darkness into his marvelous light.

To my beloved husband Ben, who patiently took on extra time with the kids and overflowing housework so that I could write this book. Words cannot express how deeply I treasure your love and unending support of my creative pursuits.

To Tristan, Vesper, and River, my treasured children, who challenge and teach me every day, and whose precious hearts I am humbled to protect.

To Seraph, my sweet heavenly child, who has taught me more about trusting in God than I ever thought possible.

To my parents, Ron and Kathy, whose unconditional love and support I am deeply grateful for every day. Thank you for bringing your child to her Savior's feet.

For Sara, who was the answered prayer for a best friend nearly fifteen years ago. Thank you for encouraging me and working with me on every adventure. I praise God for your friendship.

To the 62 women who answered my survey before I started this book. Thank you for sharing your hearts with me. I feel privileged to have been offered a glimpse into your journeys.

For the friends who experienced this book in its infant stages and gave me their feedback and encouragement: Anada, Pastor Limpert, and Paula.

And for every person along my journey who has loved, encouraged, or uplifted me. I have no words to express my thankfulness for each and every one of you.

Statement of Belief

I believe in the Triune God, (Father, Son, Spirit). I believe that I am saved by grace alone through faith in Jesus Christ, who died on the cross to erase my sins. I cannot by any effort of my own earn salvation; it is given to me as a free gift through the death and resurrection of my Savior Jesus.